“IN THEIR OWN WORDS”
THE VICTORIANS
Robert Hull

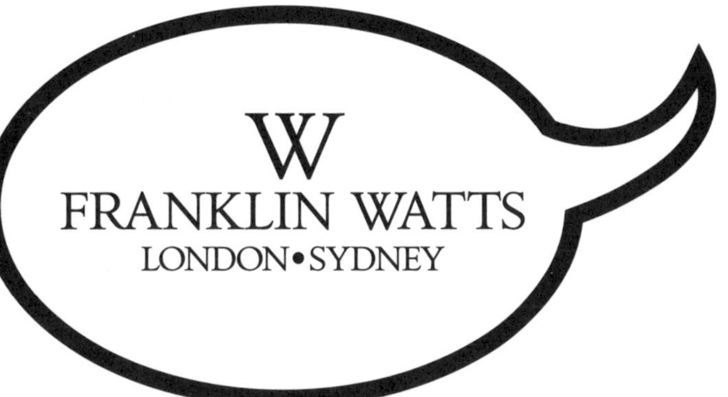
W
FRANKLIN WATTS
LONDON•SYDNEY

First published in 2001 by
Franklin Watts
96 Leonard Street
EC2A 4XD

Franklin Watts Australia
56 O'Riordan Street
Alexandria
NSW 2015

Series editor: Rachel Cooke
Editor: Sarah Ridley
Designer: Jason Anscomb
Consultant: Katherine Prior PhD (Cantab)
Illustrations: Mike White
Cover images: Mary Evans Picture Library: front & back covers bl & br.
Whilst every attempt has been made to clear copyright should there be an inadvertent omission please apply in the first instance to the publisher regarding rectification.

A CIP catalogue record for this book is available from the British Library.

ISBN 0 7496 4071 5

Dewey Classification 941.081

Printed in Malaysia

"IN THEIR OWN WORDS"

Introduction

The Victorian People

Everyday life changed greatly for millions of people in Victorian times. Between 1837, when Queen Victoria came to the throne at the age of 18, and 1901, when she died, about 9 million people left these islands for lands far away, especially Canada, the United States, Australia and New Zealand. Britain ruled some of these lands as colonies of the British Empire – an empire which, with wars and colonizing trade, grew bigger and bigger. Countries like India, Egypt and Nigeria, and a hundred smaller far-flung territories and islands were all under the rule of Queen Victoria.

In Britain itself, there was a steady drift of people from the countryside to the towns and cities. In 1837, nearly a quarter of the population worked in the countryside, but by 1901 the proportion of rural workers had dropped to about a tenth. Meanwhile the total population had just about doubled, from around 20 to around 40 million.

Because they had to house many more people, towns became more important. Some towns, especially in the north of England and Scotland, grew so quickly – from village-sized places to great cities – that squalid housing conditions developed. In many areas there was terrible overcrowding. Sanitation hardly existed; drains and streams flowed with filth. In 1849, 14,000 people died of cholera[1]. No-one then knew that the disease was carried by germs that flourished in filthy water.

Families had migrated to these towns for work because, especially early on in Queen Victoria's reign, an industrial revolution was under way, creating new mills and mines, workshops, foundries and forges. Whole families worked there, even the children, and often for very long hours in poor conditions. The landscape itself was changing, too, as huge engineering projects were completed – railways, canals, tunnels, bridges and public buildings.

In this time of change and upheaval, reformers came forward to try to remedy the worst of the evils they saw

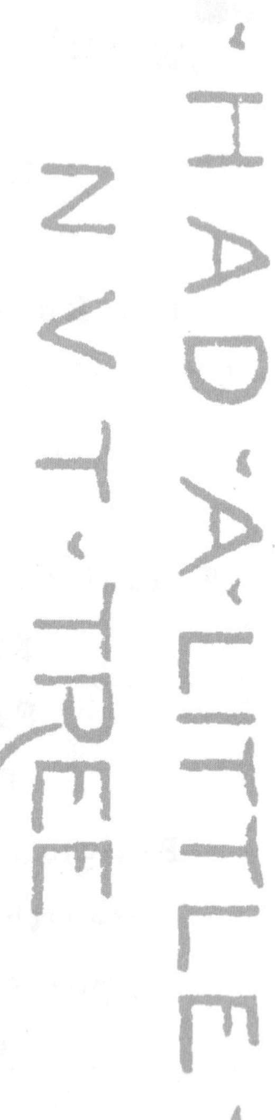

1. **cholera**: a highly infectious and often fatal disease, whose symptoms include fever, vomiting and diarrhoea.

round them. Edwin Chadwick struggled to improve housing and sanitation, starting with his report on public health in 1842, and, later on, doctors learned to connect filth with disease; they learned how disease spread, and then how to control it with antiseptics like carbolic acid. In industry, Lord Ashley and others worked to take women and children out of the mines and reduce their hours of work.

Many opposed reforms because they might affect profits. This was because British manufactured goods were sold round the world, as well as in greater and greater quantities in Britain. The production of many things which we take for granted dates from Victorian times. The Victorians made, sold and exported enormous quantities of goods large and small, from steamships, railway engines, and farm machinery, to bicycles and household cutlery.

A New Social Order

This production activity created new kinds of work. Factories, railways, export businesses, banks and insurance companies, all needed clerks, salesmen, lawyers, overseas representatives, and so on. The government itself needed more and more employees for the civil service; all the changes that were happening meant so much more law-making and so many more commissions and reports.

These were mostly jobs where people didn't get their hands dirty – middle-class jobs, seen as being different from working-class jobs in factories, workshops and as servants. The class structure now included this new middle class, between the labourer and the landed gentry[2]. These were the people who started to vote, send their children to school, keep servants, and spend money on books and clothes.

So perhaps it was not surprising that most Victorians believed in 'progress'. It was hard not to, thinking about amazing inventions such as electric lights and the motor car, great conveniences like the Penny Post[3], the speed of the new railways and the glamour of international steamships.

2. **landed gentry**: upper-class landowners.
3. **Penny Post**: the postage system introduced in 1840, where letters could be sent using postage stamps. The first stamps cost 1 penny.

Britain was the leading industrial nation, its empire was the biggest the world had ever seen. Increased prosperity and health came to many thousands of people, and more leisure and comfort. Many more men – not women yet – gained the right to vote. A beginning was made of free state schooling.

There were dark sides to Victorian progress as well. Many people didn't share in the good times. There were some bad times for agriculture and labouring country people. A terrible famine in Ireland, a cruel turning-out of thousands from their homes in the Scottish Highlands and several wars, round the world, accompanied the 'march of Empire'.

The Written Words of the Victorians

All around us is evidence of the lives and work of Victorians – bridges, tunnels, piers, embankments, canals and terraces of houses. With the invention of the camera and sound recording, innumerable photographs and some voices survive, as well as thousands of mass-produced objects.

But what is more important here is that far more of what was written down has survived. We can read thousands of private letters, journals and diaries, some written by labourers and some by factory owners. It is the working people who are usually most hidden from view as we don't tend to have a huge amount of written material by them, although we do get their words recorded through reports and surveys conducted by the government. Victorian governments also kept more records than any previous ones, like the daily logs of what happened in schools.

Many newspapers and magazines were first published in Victorian times. More novels, poems, songs and ballads were published than ever before, even children's books that had been specially written for them, like Kipling's *The Jungle Book*.

Of course many people told stories much later, in the 20th century, about their childhood in Victorian times. As these were not written at the time, we have to remember that they are being written with the benefit of hindsight.

Biographies of the Main Contributors

Lord Ashley, later Lord Shaftesbury, (1801-1885) was a tireless reformer. In 1842, he introduced a bill into Parliament, known as Lord Ashley's Act, which forbade the employment of women in mines and of children under 10.

Edwin Chadwick (1800-1890) worked to improve the sanitation and living conditions of the poor. His *The Sanitary Condition of the Labouring Population* (1842) described living conditions in Leeds and created enthusiasm for reforms.

Hannah Cullick (1833-1909) started full-time work at the age of 8 and was in domestic service most of her life. In 1854, after meeting Arthur Munby, she started to keep a diary which she continued until 1872, when she married him.

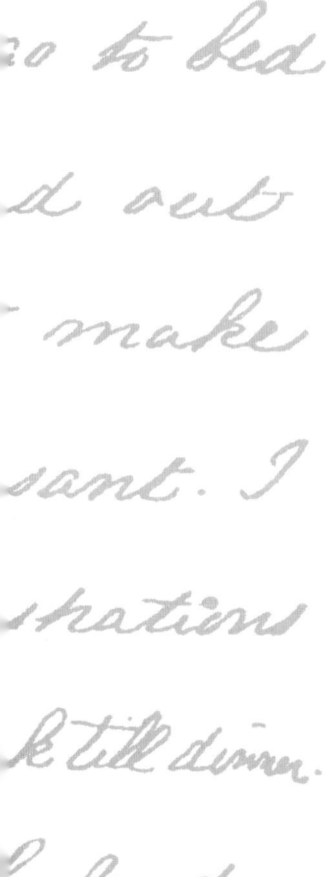

Charles Darwin (1809-1882) was educated at Cambridge. Then, in 1831, he sailed round the world as a naturalist on board *HMS Beagle*. The observations he made on the journey, especially on the Galapagos Islands, were the basis of his theory of evolution, which shook the Victorian world when *The Origin of Species by Natural Selection* was published in 1859.

Charles Dickens (1812–1870), novelist, was born into a poor family. Dickens had little schooling, then worked in a factory. Many of his novels were first published in serial form.

Henry Mayhew (1812-1887) was a journalist who wrote a collection of interviews and observations, *London Labour and the London Poor*, which highlighted the need for reform.

John Stuart Mill (1806-1873) was a philosopher and an MP. He tried, unsuccessfully, to introduce a law giving women the vote and wrote a book called *The Subjection of Women*.

Florence Nightingale (1820-1910) came from a middle-class family. Her horror at the terrible hospital conditions for soldiers wounded in the Crimean War led her to work on a Royal Commission on army health care. She became a tireless campaigner for better nursing care.

Flora Thompson (1876-1947) wrote *Lark Rise to Candleford*, about her childhood as part of a better-off working-class family in the Oxfordshire countryside in the 1880s.

Victorian Beliefs

Important changes took place in Victorian times to how people looked at themselves and the world. Many came to believe in universal suffrage[1] – the idea that everyone should have a vote in Parliamentary elections. The campaigning pressure of the Chartists, a group of people established in the 1830s demanding the vote for all, did lead to three Reform Acts. Whilst these acts gave the vote to many more people, there were exceptions, notably all women.

1. **suffrage**: a vote.

Belief in progress was a driving force in Victorian times. Victorians saw industries producing enormous quantities of new cheap goods and fast railway trains replacing slow horse-drawn coaches. For most people, it seemed life was getting better; people were growing more prosperous. Many Victorians, but not all, were pleased with their world. Others set about improving it with efforts to reform poor housing, working conditions and public health.

Democracy

The Reform Acts gave more people the right to vote in elections, but this list shows those who still could not vote.

Women; persons under twenty-one years of age; peers[2];... aliens[3], unless made denizens[4] by the Queen ... or naturalized by Act of Parliament; persons of unsound mind – idiots and lunatics; persons convicted of felony[5], bribery, perjury or petit larceny[6]; commissioners and officers of excise, customs, stamps and taxes, all persons in the employ of the post-office; police magistrates or police officers, and all persons employed in the Thames and Metropolitan Police.

Royal Kalendar and Court and City Register, 1865

2. **peer**: a member of the nobility, with a seat in the House of Lords.
3. **alien**: from a different country.
4. **made denizen**: given citizenship.
5. **felony**: a serious crime.
6. **petit larceny**: petty theft.

The Victorian philosopher, John Stuart Mill, wrote an influential book called *Representative Government*. In it he said that everyone ought to be able to vote unless there is a good reason why not. (He would exclude anyone who couldn't read or do arithmetic or pay taxes.)

Whoever, in an otherwise popular government, has no vote, and no prospect of obtaining it, will either be a permanent malcontent, or will feel as one whom the general affairs of society do not concern...
If the government makes you do things, you should have the right to a say in who the government is.

And on differences in sex, he said:

I consider it to be as entirely irrelevant to political rights, as differences in height, or the colour of the hair.

John Stuart Mill, 1861

Even those who supported votes for women were often half-hearted. Walter Shirley made this speech in 1882:

We are most of us in favour of allowing unmarried women and widows having the necessary property qualifications to vote in the election of members of Parliament. For obvious reasons, we would not accord this privilege to wives, and indeed if universal suffrage were to be carried, we should recognize the wisdom of making an arrangement to prevent the votes of men being swamped by those of women.

Walter Shirley, 1882

Exploration and Travel

With the development of the railway system in Britain and abroad, along with the introduction of steamships, travel became easier. For some Victorians this meant day trips to the seaside but others went off to Africa and the East to travel and explore.

Mary Kingsley canoed through rapids and fell in love with the African jungle. This sketch comes from her *Travels in West Africa.*

In the darkness around me flitted thousands of fireflies, and out beyond this pool of utter night flew by unceasingly the white foam of the rapids; sound there was none save their thunder.

Mary Kingsley, 1893-5

Charles Darwin set off round the world in 1831. The book he wrote as a result of his travels, *The Origin of Species by Natural Selection*, challenged the widely held view that the creation story[1] in the Bible was literally true. He put forward a theory of evolution suggesting that species change and modify themselves - their forms are not fixed. Some, like these finches, with their different-sized beaks, gave him a clue to the theory he developed later.

The remaining land-birds form a most singular group of finches, related to each other in the structure of their beaks, short tails, form of body, and plumage: there are thirteen species... All these species are peculiar to this archipelago[2]... Two species may be often seen climbing about the flowers of the great cactus-trees; but all the other species of this group of finches, mingled together in flocks, feed on the dry and sterile ground of the lower districts... The most curious fact is the perfect gradation in the size of beaks of the different species ... from one as large as a hawfinch, to that of a chaffinch.

Charles Darwin, 1835

1. **creation story**: that God created the world and all the creatures in it in just seven days.
2. **archipelago**: a group of islands.

Progress

Queen Victoria's longest-serving prime minister, William Ewart Gladstone, expressed a common belief of the times.

It is a time of rapid progress, and progress in itself is good.

W E Gladstone, 1879

Some people came to think that the positive benefits of progress were outweighed by the negative effect on the workers. Samuel Barnett, Canon[3] of the Church of England, wrote this letter after visiting a mill.

What is the good of progress if it makes the conditions of life so bare for the many that a few may have luxuries? What change has been brought about but a great increase in population?

Samuel Augustus Barnett, 1844

3. **canon**: a member of the clergy in the Church of England, often linked with a cathedral.

The Rural Working Class

We might imagine the Victorian countryside as quiet and picturesque, with villages that are pleasant to live in, each with its friendly church. But for many, life in the countryside was as hard as it was in industrial towns. Society was clearly divided into rich and poor as a large percentage of the land was held by a few upper-class landowners – four-fifths of the United Kingdom was owned by only 7,000 people. When the Earl of Yarborough died in 1875, his stock of cigars sold for £850 – more than 18 years' income for one of the labourers on his estate.

Life had become much harder for the farm labourers as they had lost their common land through enclosure[4]. The Highlands of Scotland and large areas of Ireland continued to be cleared during the Victorian era, with great hardship caused to many. There was unrest at the unfairness of this. Many families had already moved to the new industrial towns to work in mills, factories and mines, and they continued to do so. In 1851, 21.7 per cent of the population worked in agriculture, compared to 10.5 per cent in 1891.

4. **enclosure**: the process of landowners fencing off, for their own private use, farm and grazing land that had previously been common land which anyone could use.

5. **squire**: a gentleman landowner.

Village Life

Joseph Arch, a farm labourer born in 1826 who founded the National Agricultural Labourers' Union, described how everyone had their place in village life.

We labourers had no lack of lords and masters. There were the parson and his wife at the rectory. There was the squire[5], with his hand of iron over shadowing us all. There was no velvet glove on that hard hand, as many a poor man found to his hurt... At the sight of the squire the people trembled. He lorded it right feudally over his tenants. The farmers in turn tyrannised over the labourers; the labourers were no better than toads under a harrow. Most of the farmers were oppressors of the poor; they put on the iron wage-screw, and screwed the labourer's wages down, down below the living point; they stretched him on the rack of life-long abject poverty.

Joseph Arch, 1898

Country Cottages

In 1874, Richard Jefferies sketched a grim word-picture of the lives of country labourers in the south of England. One family he visited went to bed at half-past five in order to save fuel and candles.

The rain comes through the hole in the thatch, the mud floor is damp, and perhaps sticky. If the floor is of uneven stones, these grow damp and slimy. The cold wind comes through the ill-fitting sash, and drives with terrible force under the door... Inside, the draught is only one degree better than the smoke. These low chimneys, overshadowed with trees, fill the room endlessly with smother... Here the family are all huddled up closely over the embers. Here the cooking is done, such as it is. Here they sit in the dark.

Richard Jefferies, 1874

There were compassionate landowners who wished to improve rural housing. When Lord Ashley inherited his Dorset estate in 1851, he made this note in his diary:

Inspected few cottages – filthy, close, indecent, unwholesome. Shocking state of cottages; stuffed like pigs in a drum. Were not the people cleanly as they can be, we should have had an epidemic. Must build others, cost what it may!

Unfortunately, his estate was in debt.

Surely I am the most perplexed of men. I have passed my life in berating others for rotten houses and immoral, filthy dwellings; and now I come to an estate rife with abominations! Why, there are things here to make one's flesh creep; and I have not a farthing[1] to set them right.

But he did find money to build some cottages, start cricket clubs, and give prizes for the best-kept allotments.

It is far better to have a well-inhabited well-cottaged property, people in decency and comfort, than well-hung walls[2] which persons seldom see.

Lord Ashley, 1851

1. **farthing**: a fourth of a penny. See note 3.
2. **well-hung walls**: walls covered with expensive paintings.

Feeding the Family

Many labourers' families in the 1880s took home less than 10 shillings[3] a week to feed the family. Bread and beer was the main diet, supplemented by the odd piece of pork or rabbits stolen from the squire[4]. The diet of labourers like J Barwick, born in 1886, was often poor, or monotonous.

When I was, as I say, in plough service, I lived on fat pork[5] for twelve month. That's all we had. Bar Sundays. Used to have a beef pudding. But that's all I had for breakfast, dinner and tea. Fat pork.

J Barwick c. 1910

3. **shilling**: a unit of old money. There were 12 pennies (d) in a shilling; and 20 shillings (s) in a pound (£). £1 in 1850 would today be worth £55.
4. **squire**: see page 11.
5. **fat pork**: this doesn't refer to the pork meat, but simply to the lard or pork fat which would have been eaten with bread.

In contrast, wealthy and middle-class people who lived in the countryside, like this army officer's family in the 1860s, lived and ate well enough.

We always had a Sunday dinner of roast beef, Yorkshire pudding, roasted potatoes, vegetables, and apple tart in summer and plum pudding in winter, and on the side-table a row of jam pots into which slices of beef and its accompaniments were put. A paper was then tied over each and they were removed from the kitchen, from whence old people or children fetched them for the refreshment of village invalids.

Bernice Baker, c. 1860

Poaching

In the hard times of the 1840s, when his own father was out of work and couldn't feed the family, James Hawker turned to poaching[6]. Many poorer families did poach but it was illegal and, if caught, the poacher could be sent to Australia as a punishment. In his private journals, published long after his death, Hawker described his first attempts at finding food.

We went to live in a very poor part of the town. In this year 1850 – when I was 14 years of age – I first commenced to poach. My father had tried to better our position lawfully

6. **poaching**: the illegal hunting of game or fish. The animals are the property of the person who owns the land or river.

and had failed. So I was determined to try some other means. I was surrounded by every temptation. The class that starved me certainly tempted me with all their game and fish. Having no gun, no net, no dog, I was content for a time to poach fish with a ball of string hooks and small baits. I would catch pike ranging from one to ten pounds [approx. 0.5 to 5kg] each.

James Hawker, c. 1880

Forced Off the Land

Most land in England had been enclosed[1] in the late 18th and early 19th century. In the Highlands of Scotland, this process continued through the Victorian period, in order for landowners to create huge areas for sheep farming.

1. **enclosure**: see page 11.

A Glasgow lawyer, Donald Ross, came to see for himself what was happening, and wrote newspaper articles about it.

The poor tailor they made short work of. They found him quietly sitting down to his breakfast, when they seized him and pitched him outside the door, sending his humble breakfast after him. They next turned on his wife, who was lying sick in bed. They dragged her from her bed screaming, and set her outside, bruising and discolouring her arm. Her infant child, who was sucking at her breast, was taken and laid upon the ground. All their effects were thrown out after them, and the door locked.

Donald Ross, 1859

The supporters of Highland clearances justified them as 'improvements'. James Loch, Commissioner for the Marquess of Stafford's estates in Scotland, created the Policy of Improvement, and writes this about it.

The adoption of the new system, by which the mountainous districts are converted into sheep pastures, even if it should unfortunately occasion the emigration of some individuals, is, upon the whole, advantageous to the nation at large.

James Loch, 1815

In Ireland absentee English and Irish landowners kept most of the Irish people in a state of rural poverty. Matters were made worse by the failure of the potato crop in successive years (see page 33). Tenant farmers and labourers who could not pay the rent were evicted from the land.

In the county of Clare the clearance system is still in vigorous operation, notwithstanding the vast numbers evicted during the last three years. The **Limerick and Clare Examiner** ***of Saturday states that "seventy families, amounting to probably three hundred and seventy souls, had been evicted from the property of Colonel Wyndham, in the parish of Clondegad."***

The article continued:

Their dwellings have been left, with few exceptions – in the words of our correspondent – hideous heaps of ruins... There is no room for the crowd at the Ennis union workhouse[2]. They are denied outdoor relief, on some pretext or other. Women, with their infants in their arms, slept out under the freezing cold of the past week, and the floor of the chapel is now the only home of the exterminated people.

The London Illustrated News, 1849

2. **workhouse**: an institution where the poor were housed, often in prison-like conditions, and given work to do.

From 1879, the Irish Land League retaliated against landowners. Charles Parnell, its President, decided that farmers should refuse to farm the land left clear after eviction. Parnell later went on to campaign for Home Rule for Ireland.

When a man takes a farm from which another has been evicted you must shun him on the roadside when you meet him – you must shun him in the streets of the town – you must shun him in the shop – you must shun him in the fair-green and in the market-place, and even in the place of worship.

Charles Parnell, 1880

The Industrial Working Class

In the hundred years before Victoria came to the throne, the Industrial Revolution had caused a complete change in working life. In the course of around 80 years, inventors had found ways of using steam power (produced by burning coal) to drive all kinds of machinery, to make wool and cotton goods, and to power locomotive engines on railways, and boats on rivers, lakes and seas.

Families left the countryside and flocked into the towns and cities to work in mines, mills and factories. While the mills made cotton and woollen goods for a world market – and wealth for their owners – poverty, ill-health and despair followed for many workers. In many cases, the cities and towns were growing so fast that the living standards of these urban people became appalling.

Coal-mining

The factories depended on coal, mined from far under the ground in coal fields in Wales, Scotland and northern England. Not just men, but women and young children worked in the mines. After the Mines Act of 1844 women and children under 10 were not supposed to work underground – but they did, though less and less as time went on.

A writer for a London magazine described life underground in 1862.

In a small corner-like recess, full of floating coal-dust, foul and noisome with bad air and miscellaneous refuse and garbage, glimmer three or four Davy lamps*[1]*. Close and deliberate scrutiny will discover one hewer nearly naked lying on his back, elevating his short sharp pickaxe a little above his nose, and picking into the coal-seam with might and main.

The London Illustrated News, 1862

1. **Davy lamp**: a safety-lamp used in coal-mines, invented by Sir Humphry Davy (1778-1829).

In 1842, one woman of 40 told a Commission enquiring into conditions in Scottish mines how she had worked in the pit since she was 7.

I have worked underground for 33 years. I have had 9 children and two dead born, which was due to the work. I have always had to work till the birth, and return after 10 or 12 days.

Government Report, 1842

An 11-year-old girl also spoke to the Commission.

I work with my father and have done so for two years. Father starts at two in the morning. I start with the women at 5 and come up at 5 at night. I work all night on Fridays, and come up at 12 on Saturdays. I carry coal from the face to the pit-bottom.

Six members of the family work with father below. When work is good he takes away £1 to £1 2s 5d[2] a week.

Government Report, 1842

2. £1 2s 5d: This works out as a little under £60 per year – worth about £2,700 in today's money. See also page 13.

Life in the Towns

Charles Dickens went north to Preston to see what a growing, modern industrial town was like. He didn't like what he saw, as this extract from his novel *Hard Times* shows.

It was a town of red brick, or brick that would have been red if the smoke and ashes had allowed it; but as matters stood it was a town of unnatural red and black like the painted face of a savage. It was a town of machinery and tall chimneys, out of which interminable serpents of smoke trailed themselves for ever and ever, and never got uncoiled. It had a black canal in it, and a river that ran purple with ill-smelling dye, and vast piles of buildings full of windows where there was a rattling and a trembling all day long, and where the piston of the steam-engine worked up and down like the head of an elephant in a state of melancholy madness.

Charles Dickens, 1854

Hours at the Mill

It was a long day in the mills, starting perhaps at 4.30am with the watchman's call. In 1841, a writer saw for himself what the day was like for a young woman mill-worker.

The clock strikes half-past five. The engine starts, and her day's work commences.
At half-past seven, the engine slacks its pace ... for a short time, till the hands have cleaned the machinery and swallowed a little food. It then goes on again, and continues at full speed till twelve o'clock, when it stops for dinner. Before leaving the factory, and in her dinner hour, she has her machines to clean.
After dinner, which she seldom has time to eat, it is time to be on her way to work again, where she remains, without one minute's relaxation, till seven o'clock. Then she comes home, and throws herself into a chair, exhausted.

Journalist, 1841

Factories punished workers for lateness and time-wasting. In 1844, James Leach, a weaver in a Manchester cotton mill, showed these rules to the MP James Rashleigh.

1. The door of the lodge will be closed ten minutes after the engine starts every morning, and no weaver will afterwards be admitted till breakfast-time. Any weaver who may be absent during that time shall forfeit three-pence[1] per loom.
2. Weavers absent at any other time when the engine is working, will be charged three-pence per hour each loom for such absence; and weavers leaving the room without the consent of the over-looker, shall forfeit three-pence...
9. All shuttles, brushes, oil-cans, wheels, windows etc if broken shall be paid for by the weaver...
11. Any mill-hand who is seen talking to another, whistling or singing, will be fined sixpence.

Mill Rules, 1844

1. **three-pence**: see page 13.

Many people could see the unpleasant aspects of the factory system. In 1831, Robert Owen's *New View of Society* explained his aims to improve life for the workers at his New Lanark factory. In early Victorian times, Owen's example led others to reconsider their attitudes towards factory life.

The practice of employing children in the mills of six, seven and eight years of age was discontinued, and their parents advised to allow them to acquire health and education until they were ten years old. The children were taught reading, writing and arithmetic during five years, that is, from five to ten, without expense to their parents... During the period that these changes were going forward, attention was given to the domestic arrangements of the community. Their houses were rendered more comfortable, their streets were improved, the best provisions were purchased and sold to them at low rates.

Robert Owen, 1831

The Sweat-shop System

Sweated labour was a system where the workers had to buy their own materials and equipment, say cloth and a sewing machine, and were only paid for the items they made, regardless of how long each piece took to finish. These were then sold at a vast profit by the owner of the sweat-shop.

This woman – answering questions at a government enquiry into the 'sweating system' in 1888 – describes how each time she fell behind with payments on a sewing machine, she lost all the money she had already paid.

Will you describe to the committee the nature of your work?

I make shirts at 7d and 8d a dozen. I have to pay for my own cotton out of it, and I have to pay 2s 6d a week for the machine. And I have to pay half a crown[2] a week on the hiring system.

How many shirts can you make in a day?

Two dozen; and I have little children to attend to.

2. **crown**: a 5s coin. See page 13.

Two dozen a day? at 7d a dozen? That is 1s 2d a day? What have you to find?

A reel of cotton and oil for my machine out of that. About 1s 3d a week.

Who do you get your machine from?

Messrs Singer & Company.

Does it become your property after a time?

Yes – £7 3s I have to pay.

What happens if you get into arrears?

They will take it all away from me. I am in arrears now with my machine.

If you are a certain time in arrears you lose all that you have paid upon it?

Yes.

Has that ever happened to you?

Yes.

Government Report, 1888

All Kinds of Work

Hundreds of jobs that are now the work of machines or robots had to be done by hand in Victorian times. Street-lamps were lit by lamplighters and boy chimney sweeps climbed up the chimneys to clean them. Thousands of people worked as household servants for the wealthier families.

In the 1840s and 50s, the journalist Henry Mayhew gathered a great deal of information about the lives of London's working people. At first it was published in weekly instalments in *The Morning Chronicle* newspaper. It showed the huge variety of working-class jobs in the city.

I am informed ... that there are 18,000 itinerant sellers of fish, vegetables and fruit in the metropolis... There are supposed to be at least 500 sellers of water-cresses; 200 coffee stalls; 300 cats' meat men; 250 ballad singers; 200 play-bill sellers; from 800 to 1000 bone-grubbers[1] and mudlarks[2]; 1000 crossing-sweepers; another 1000 chimney

1. **bone-grubber**: someone who collects bones from rubbish to sell to make glue.
2. **mudlark**: someone who makes a living by scavenging for things washed up on the banks of tidal rivers, in this case the Thames.

3. **turncock**: a person responsible for regulating the supply of water from the mains to houses and street pumps.

sweeps, and the same number of turncocks[3] and lamplighters.

Henry Mayhew, 1849

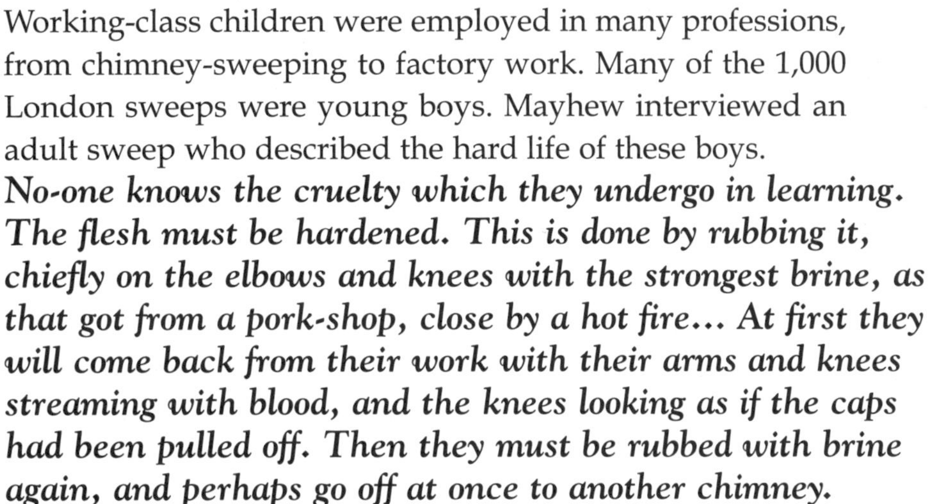

Children at Work

Working-class children were employed in many professions, from chimney-sweeping to factory work. Many of the 1,000 London sweeps were young boys. Mayhew interviewed an adult sweep who described the hard life of these boys.

No-one knows the cruelty which they undergo in learning. The flesh must be hardened. This is done by rubbing it, chiefly on the elbows and knees with the strongest brine, as that got from a pork-shop, close by a hot fire... At first they will come back from their work with their arms and knees streaming with blood, and the knees looking as if the caps had been pulled off. Then they must be rubbed with brine again, and perhaps go off at once to another chimney.

Henry Mayhew, 1849

Factory workers and their children were constantly exposed to danger from unguarded machines. This inspector reported the indifference of one workshop owner to children's safety.

Little boys and girls are here seen at work at the tip-punching machines, all acting by steam-power with their fingers in constant danger of being punched off once in every second, while the same time they have their heads between the whirling wheels a few inches distant from each ear. "They seldom lose a hand," said one of the proprietors to me, in explanation; "it only takes off a finger at the first or second joint. Sheer carelessness! Looking about them – sheer carelessness!"

Government Report, 1843

came to vi - sit me, And all for the sake of my lit -tle nut - tree.

Gradually Factory Acts began to improve the life of working people. An Act of Parliament in 1844 was a step towards real improvement for children.

And be it enacted that no child shall be employed in any factory more than six hours and thirty minutes in any one day.

Factory Act, 1844

Self-help for the Working Classes

To help each other, working people organized 'mutual assistance' societies, like the one Samuel Smiles describes in his very popular book, *Self-Help: With Illustrations of Character and Conduct*. The book sold in enormous numbers, and was translated into many languages.

The working people of Leeds alone subscribed not less than £15,000[1] annually for mutual assistance against sickness and accident. Ten shillings was paid weekly to a member while sick; medical attendance was also provided; £10 was allowed on the death of a member, and £5 to the widow.

Samuel Smiles, 1859

1. £15,000: worth over £800,000 today. See page 13.

The idea of unions was for workers to band together to avoid being exploited by employers. In the year of Victoria's death, 1901, Ralph Blumenfeld recorded in his diary a revealing conversation with a bus driver.

I had a prolonged chat with an [horse] omnibus driver all the way from the City to Sloane Square. The old man must be over seventy, but looks quite young. They now have a 'Busmen's Union', and they are beginning to agitate for a day off now and then without being fired for it. They work 365 days a year, and think that too much.

Ralph Blumenfeld, 1901

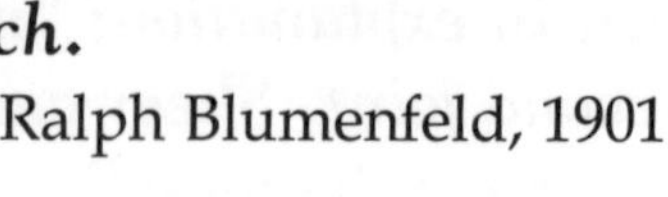

A New Middle Class

Victorian factories, importing cheap raw materials from Britain's colonies, made goods to sell round the world. With developing trade and commerce, a large middle class grew up, separate from the aristocratic classes 'above' them, and the working classes 'below'. Many of them earned less than £100 a year – no more than the better-paid factory worker, but they believed in hard work, and getting on.

If they ever became well-off, there was the hope of being accepted by 'society'[2] people, or much better-paid professional people – army officers and lawyers, for instance. In turn, these upper-middle-class people aspired to join the upper class – a difficult job as society formed strict rules on this. Equally, a growing number of the working classes began to aspire to middle-class ideas of prosperity and respectability. To be 'respectable' was to be God-fearing, good-mannered and correctly dressed – and to be able to afford to live in one of the new town houses, send your children to school and enjoy some of the Victorian luxuries of life.

2. **'society'**: in this case, the elite group of mainly upper-class, wealthy people who set the fashions of the day and who socialize together.

Middle-class, Respectable Jobs

It was the job or career of the father of the family that usually gave the family its class status. Middle-class jobs included the steady, respectable jobs in shipping, insurance, banks, law-offices, shops and the growing civil service. Most of these jobs paid better than factory work.

Thousands of young men were clerks in business offices. To 'get on' as a clerk you had to be respectable, as these stern rules from *Office Staff Practice* show.

Clothing must be of a sober nature. The clerical staff will not disport themselves in raiment of bright colour...
The craving for tobacco, wines or spirits is a human weakness, and is forbidden.
No talking is allowed during business hours.

Office Staff Practice, 1852

Aspiring Upwards

Victorian people were preoccupied with the levels of society[1]. They had to 'know their place', but the *Etiquette Book* also stressed the need to 'rise' socially.

Always seek the society[2] of those above yourself… The man who is content to seek associates in his own grade (unless his station be very exalted) will always be in danger of retrograding. What is good company? It is composed of persons of birth, rank, fashion and respectability.

Arthur Freeling, 1840

1. **society**: in this context, the whole of the population.
2. **society**: here, the people you spend your time with.
3. **'society'**: see page 23.

Wealthy Victorian businessmen often had difficulty getting into real 'society'[3]. They were still only 'middle class', as a novelist, Walter Besant, recalled.

But men in 'trade' – bankers were still accounted tradesmen – could not possibly belong to society. That is to say, if they went to live in the country they were not called upon by the county families, and in town they were not admitted by the men into their clubs, or by ladies into their houses.

Walter Besant, 1887

Daisy Ashford wrote her nicely mis-spelled novel, *The Young Visiters*, when she was 9. She could see adults round her trying to 'get on' in society. Her hero, Mr Salteena, is:

… an elderly man of 42 … not quite a gentleman but you would hardly notice.

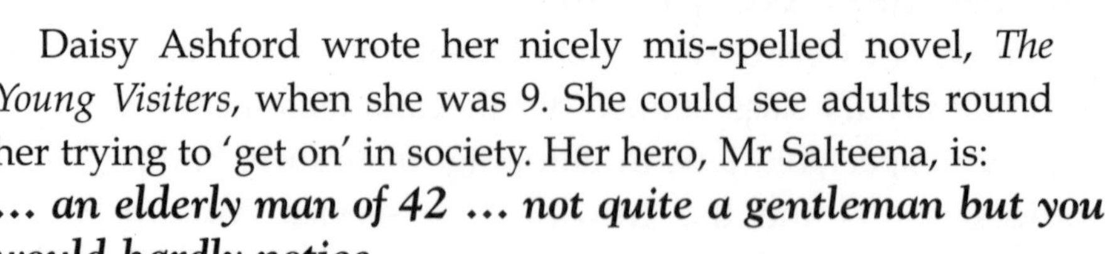

His father was a butcher, so he pretends that his mother is an upper-class lady.

Unfortunately, "he is not quite the right side of the blanket", as they say, in fact he is the son of a first rate butcher but his mother was from a decent family called Hyssops of the Glen so you see he is not so bad and is desireus of being the correct article.

Daisy Ashford, c. 1860

Learning to Laugh

Good table-manners were essential for claiming a place in society; not everyone knew the rules so people made money by publishing books on the subject. In *Manners for Women*, 'Madge of Truth' (Mrs C E Humphry) said that women needed to learn not only when to 'rise from the table' and leave the men to chat, but also how to laugh properly.

Miss Florence St John told the world once in the pages of a Sunday newspaper how she learnt to laugh. Mr Farnie, she says, took her in hand for the laughing scene in **Madame Favart*****, and made her sing a descending octave staccato with the syllables "Ha! Ha!" The actress rehearsed it over and over again... Anyone who has heard Miss St John's pretty laugh on the stage will admit it was worth taking some pains to achieve... Laughing should, if its expression does not come by nature, be carefully taught.***

Mrs C E Humphry, 1897

And in her *Manners for Men*, 'Madge' related a terrible error.

In dealing with bread, use neither knife nor fork. It must be broken with the fingers. There is a story of an absent-minded and short-sighted prelate[4] who, with the remark, "My bread, I think?" dug his fork into the white hand of a lady who sat beside him.

Mrs C E Humphry, 1897

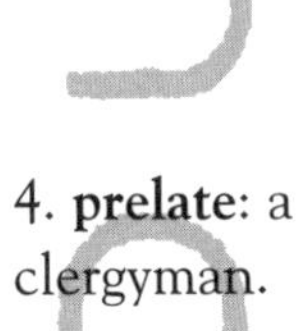

4. **prelate**: a clergyman.

Middle-class Home Life

The brothers George and Weedon Grossmith gently made fun of the lifestyle of 'respectable' lower-middle-class people, who could just afford a servant and a piano, in *The Diary of a Nobody*. It was supposedly kept by Mr Pooter.

My dear wife Carrie and I have just been a week in our new house, 'The Laurels', Brickfield Terrace, Holloway – a very nice six-roomed residence, not counting basement, with a front breakfast parlour. We have a little front garden, and

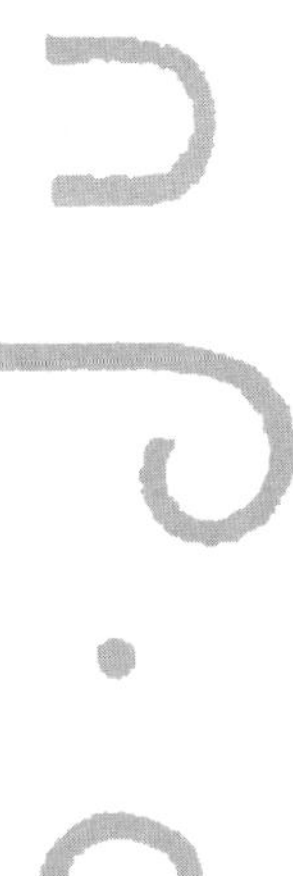

there is a flight of ten steps up to the front door, which, by the by, we keep locked with the chain up. Cummings, Gower, and our other intimate friends always come up to the little side entrance, which saves the servant the trouble of going up to the front door, thereby taking her from her work. We have a nice little back-garden which runs down to the railway…

In the evenings, after work:

There is always something to be done; a tin-tack here, a venetian blind to put straight, a fan to nail up, or part of a carpet to nail down – all of which I can do with my pipe in my mouth; while Carrie is not above putting a button on a shirt, mending a pillow-case or practising the 'Sylvia Gavotte' on our new cottage piano (on the three years' system[1]).

George and Weedon Grossmith, 1892

1. **three years' system**: paid for in installments over the course of three years.

For well-off middle- and upper-class people, prosperity meant a large house, servants, plenty to spend on furnishings, fine clothes and good food. Having a number of servants made it easier to bring up children, keep the house clean and have a busy social life. In 1851, an American girl, Anna Fray, visiting her English uncle in Shropshire, wrote a letter home with a description of this wealthy family's organized day.

We rise early at half past eight, and breakfast a quarter of an hour later. After breakfast the children go to their schoolroom and Maria gives Kitty a music lesson. Aunt Catherine and I write or sew till eleven or twelve, when we go out driving. Uncle Richard either goes shooting by himself or with Mr Betton… We lunch when we return, and at six we dine. In the evening we form a very cheerful party by the drawing-room fire, reading, or sewing, or playing games with the children.

Anna Fray, 1851

The Great Exhibition

Through much of the Victorian period, Britain was the leading manufacturing nation of the world. To celebrate this, a huge exhibition of the 'industry and art of all nations of the earth', as Queen Victoria described it in her journal, was held in Hyde Park in London in 1851. Visitors were equally amazed by the iron and glass building, the Crystal Palace, that housed the Great Exhibition, as by what was in it. Everybody came, from dukes and earls to factory workers and farm-labourers. Trains and steamboats brought people from far away to marvel and take notes.

The Art and Industry of the World

Victoria's husband, Prince Albert, was the inspiration behind the Great Exhibition of 1851. The proud young Queen attended the opening on 1st May and returned again and again to view different displays, as she recorded in her journal.

May 1 – The tremendous cheering, the joy expressed on every face, the vastness of the building, with all its decorations and exhibits, the sound of the organ (with 200 instruments and 600 voices, which seemed nothing) and my beloved husband, the creator of this peace festival, "uniting the industry and art of all nations of the earth," all this was indeed moving, and a day to live forever...

June 7 – To the Exhibition: went to the machinery part, where we remained 2 hours, and which is excessively interesting and instructive, and fills one with admiration for the greatness of man's mind...

July 9 – We went to the Exhibition and had the electric telegraph show explained and demonstrated before us. It is the most wonderful thing, and the boy who works it does so with the greatest ease and rapidity...

July 12 – A very hot day. We went to the Exhibition – to the Gallery on the south side, going through all the exhibits of the Spitalfields silks and velvets, all the Coventry ribbons and lace from Devonshire, Nottingham, Ireland etc...

Oct. 14 – After breakfast started for the Exhibition... It looked so beautiful and I could not believe that it was the last time I should behold this wonderful creation of my beloved Albert's...

Queen Victoria, 1851

To the visitors, the 'Crystal Palace' was like a great temple to 'progress'. And much was changing; *The Economist* magazine asked readers to imagine life fifty years earlier.

We should find ourselves ... paying five-fold for our cotton handkerchiefs and stockings; receiving our Edinburgh letters in London a week after they were written ... exchanging the instantaneous telegraph for the slow and costly express by chaise and pair[1]; travelling with soreness and fatigue by the 'old heavy' coach at the rate of seven miles an hour, instead of by the Great Western [railway] at fifty.

The Economist, 1851

1. **chaise and pair**: a carriage pulled by two horses.

Charlotte Bronte was impressed by the Great Exhibition.

Whatever human industry has created you find there... It seems as if only magic could have gathered this mass of wealth from all the ends of the earth.

Charlotte Bronte, 1851

The Exhibition would not have been such an enormous success without railways and steamboats. That is clear from an entry in *The Cyclopaedia of Useful Arts*, compiled the same year.

Enormous excursion trains daily poured their thousands into the city... Large numbers of work-people received holidays for the purpose... 800 agricultural labourers in their peasants' attire from Surrey and Sussex, conducted by their clergy, at a cost of 2s 2d[2] each person – numerous firms in the north sent their people, who must have been gratified by the sight of their own handiwork – an agricultural implement maker in Suffolk sent his people in two hired vessels, provided with sleeping berths, cooling apparatus and every comfort...

Charles Tomlinson, 1851

2. **2s 2d**: see page 13.

Travel and Communications

The Victorian era was one of great inventiveness. Victorian engineers shaped the landscape we see today, building railways, tunnels, bridges, canal cuttings, viaducts and embankments, many of which are still in use. At the end of the Victorian period, the motor car was invented.

Michael Faraday's experiments with electricity in the 1830s led to the invention of the telephone in 1876. Rowland Hill developed the basis of the modern postal service. It was an age of advance and improvement.

The Railways

Many people were extremely excited by the railways, as shown in this description written by Frederick Williams. He had been allowed to ride on the foot-plate (of the engine) of the first Midland train between Bedford and London in 1869.

The train, spic and span new – the lot worth perhaps £5,000 – was standing one Monday morning on the new rails by the new platform, under the new glass and iron shed... Soon we are running on the summit of another long embankment, from which we can see the line far before us, and the country far round us. Occasionally, a group of plate-layers[3] part to the right and left of us to allow us to pass; the village girls pause upon the country road, and shade their bright faces from the sun as they gaze upon the first train that has ever run that way; the old farmer rests his arms on the top of the homestead gate ... now and then a partridge rises and whirrs away.

Frederick Williams, 1876

3. **plate-layers**: railway-builders.

Many hated the railways for the way they changed the landscape and there was opposition to railway-building. Samuel Smiles, in a biography of George and Robert Stephenson, described railway surveyors arriving on the land of Lord Sefton, a great canal proprietor. The site was blockaded, and gamekeepers fired guns to keep them off.

But the determined surveyors had a neat answer.

Some men set off guns in a particular quarter … all the gamekeepers made off in that direction. It enabled a rapid survey to be made during their absence.

Samuel Smiles, 1857

Safety on the Railways

'What speed was it safe to travel at?' was a hot topic at the start of rail travel. According to Smiles, George Stephenson thought a train's top speed ought to be 40 miles an hour[1].

I do not like either 40 or 50 miles an hour upon any line – I think it an unnecessary speed; and if there is danger upon a railway it is high velocity that creates it. I should say no railway ought to exceed forty miles an hour on the most favourable gradient; but upon a curved line the speed ought not to exceed 25 miles an hour.

Samuel Smiles, 1857

1. **40 miles per hour**: 64 km per hour. Today's trains run at speeds of up to 160 km per hour.

In 1878, the Tay Bridge was opened over the River Forth. In December 1879, it collapsed while a passenger train was crossing in a fierce storm and many people died. The popular poet-entertainer, William MacGonagall, wrote about it.

It must have been an awful sight,
To witness in the dusky moonlight,
While the Storm Fiend did laugh, and angry did bray,
Along the Railway Bridge of the silvery Tay.
Oh! ill-fated bridge of the silvery Tay,
I must now conclude my lay
By telling you fearlessly without the least dismay,
That your central girders would not have given way,
At least many sensible men do say,
Had they been supported on each side with buttresses,
At least many sensible men confesses,
For the stronger our houses we do build,
The less chance we have of being killed.

William MacGonagall, 1879

New Inventions

Up until the 1880s, people travelled on foot or by horse, boat or train. The revolutionary motor car was invented in 1885/86. In the Victorian period, motor cars were strictly limited to the wealthy. An early motor car advertisement stressed its superiority to the horse-drawn carriage.

Fifteen reasons why AN AUTOCAR
is better than a horse-drawn vehicle:
Because
It needs no stable – the coach-house is enough.
It needs no daily grooming, consequently.
No man need be kept specially to look after it,
There is no manure heap to poison the air.
It cannot shy, kick or run away.
It has no will of its own to thwart the wishes of its driver and cause disaster.
It consumes only when working, and then in exact proportion to the work done.
It cannot fall sick and die.
It will travel as fast as any one [horse].
It can be stopped with certainty and safety in twice the distance.
No cruelty is inflicted by climbing a steep hill a full load
Nor can distress be caused by high-speed travelling.

Advertisement, c. 1890

Alexander Graham Bell showed the world his new invention, the telephone, at the Philadelphia Exhibition in 1876. A journalist for *The Times*, expressed amazement.

We publish in another column the extraordinary new uses of which this invention has been found capable. By its means the human voice can be conveyed in full force from any one point to another five miles off, and with some loss of power to a very much more considerable distance still.

The Times, 1876

The early telephone only worked in one direction. This first phone conversation in England, between two engineers demonstrating it at Plymouth in 1877, needed two machines. The first engineer said:

"Hey diddle-diddle, the cat and fiddle... Now, please follow that up"...

Then, he heard the reply on the second telephone:

"There he goes – he says – 'the cow jumped over the moon'."

Record of first phone call in England, 1877

In 1840, Rowland Hill, with others helping, persuaded Parliament to adopt the cheap Penny Post[1] for letters, using pre-sold stamps for the sender to stick on. He initially described his ideas in an 1837 report for the government, *Postal Reform; its Importance and Practibility.*

Perhaps this difficulty (of using stamped envelopes in certain cases) might be obviated by using a bit of paper, just large enough to bear the stamp and covered at the back with a glutinous wash, which the bringer might, by the application of a little moisture, attach to the back of the letter...

Rowland Hill, 1837

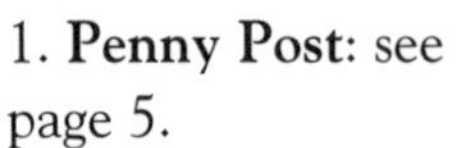

1. **Penny Post**: see page 5.

The postage stamp only became compulsory in 1853. Henry Cole, an historian, wrote:

Of all the events with which my career has been connected no one surpasses ... the adoption of a Uniform Penny Postage ... the glory of England for all time.

Henry Cole, 1886

Emigration

Queen Victoria reigned over a huge British Empire, including the vast countries of Australia, Canada, New Zealand and South Africa. Approximately three million people emigrated from the islands of Great Britain between 1837 and 1901 to these colonies and a further six million elsewhere (including the USA). Many went on an adventure, drawn to a new life in these 'new countries'. Thousands more went because they were driven to it by misery and poverty in many parts of England, a terrible famine in Ireland, and land enclosures[2] in the Highlands of Scotland.

2. enclosure: see page 11.

The Irish Famine

Hundreds of thousands of Irish people left their country in the 1840s. In 1845 and 1846, the potato crop, their main food, was destroyed by disease and a full-scale famine occurred. Nearly a million people died whilst thousands of others fled the country. Between 1849 and 1852, almost 60,000 Irish peasant farmers were evicted from their property because they could not pay the rent as a result of the crop failures. Between 1840 and 1860, an estimated two million Irish people emigrated to North America.

Thousands of Irish people with no money or belongings came on boats to England, usually to Liverpool, as Evan David of the Board of Governors of Cardiff Union described.

[They were] brought over as ballast[3], without any payment for their passage... Captains find it cheaper to ship and unship this living ballast than one of lime or shingle.

Evan David, c. 1846-7

3. ballast: heavy load needed to steady a ship in the water.

The Constable of Liverpool crossed to Ireland to find out why so many people were coming to England.

They encountered thousands of men, women and children on the high roads, moving towards the seaside for the purpose of embarking to England, most of them begging their way, and all apparently in a state of great destitution.

Constable of Liverpool, 1847

ERS' UNION

For decades afterwards, Irish people continued to emigrate in search of a better life. Jessop Hulton made this observation in his diary when he was travelling through America in 1874. He encounters Irish emigrants on a train crossing the United States.

All seemed happy. In fact there is a general air of satisfaction, very different from 'the Old Countries', probably owing to the knowledge that by honest work a man is bound to get on in this developing county of Wyoming[1].

Jessop Hulton, 1874

1. **Wyoming**: state of the USA.

Emigration

People who wanted to emigrate to improve their standard of living chose between North America, Australia, New Zealand and South Africa. Official emigration to British colonies was controlled by companies set up by the colonial governments. The person or family had to apply to one of the companies and each case was considered individually. Some colonies offered free places on ships to the new lands; others offered to help with the cost of the fare (an assisted place).

After this favourable report, the Welch family were selected for emigration to New Zealand.

The 2 eldest girls can milk and make butter – the eldest boys work occasionally – the education of the children has been well attended to. All are remarkably healthy and robust. All except the youngest have been vaccinated, had the whooping cough and the measles. Welch has such a perfect general knowledge of all kinds of out-of-door labour that I consider him one of the best of his class I have yet met with. He will pay for the 6 children under age.

Emigration Report, c. 1860-70

Emigrant Ships

On private voyages to the USA, where the government did not look after the emigrants, conditions could be bad. Most

2. **steerage**: third-class travel with sleeping quarters near the rudder of the ship.
3. **cholera**: see page 4.

people travelled steerage[2]. Of the 29 ships that left for the USA in November 1853, over 1,000 passengers out of about 14,000 died. This is from a report in *The Times*.

The emigrant is shown a berth, a shelf of coarse pinewood in a noisome dungeon, airless and lightless, in which several persons of both sexes and all ages are stowed away, on shelves two feet one inch above one another, three feet wide and six feet long, still reeking from the ineradicable stench left by the emigrants on the last voyage... After a few days have been spent in the pestilential atmosphere created by the festering mass of squalid humanity imprisoned between the damp and steaming decks, the scourge breaks out, and to the miseries of filth, foul air and darkness is added the cholera[3]. Amid hundreds of men, women and children dressing and undressing, quarrelling, fighting, cooking and drinking, one hears the groans and screams of a patient in the last agonies of this plague.

The Times, 1854

Conditions varied. The Wade family from Leicestershire were government-assisted emigrants to Australia. They wrote this letter to their relatives back in England after their journey.

During the voyage we had good food and every accommodation that could be expected on board a ship. You might bring some flour as perhaps you will not be able to eat biscuit while you are sick and cheese or anything you like. There is as much as you will eat but you will not regret as you may sell them for twice as much as you gave... Tis just as well to go free as we had just the same treatment as those who paid their passage as for being in bondage it is quite false as we are just as when at home. You pays the Board[4] which is no inconvenience whatever.

Thomas and Maria Wade, 1840

4. **Board**: Colonial Land and Emigration Commission.

The arrival of steamships changed emigrants' experience. By the mid 1860s, the journey to America took 12 to 14 days. It had previously been up to 6 weeks.

Family Life

Queen Victoria married her beloved Albert shortly after her Coronation. She had nine children in all and the royal image of happy family life became a model for middle- and upper-class families. Of course, prosperity hadn't come to all in Victorian times. Working-class families often struggled along in cramped, unhealthy conditions. With the parents and even children working such long hours, family life could hardly be said to exist.

All women's family lives were affected by their legal position. Until 1879 a husband could legally beat his wife and until 1891 he could lock her up. He owned all her earnings until 1870, and all her possessions until 1882.

The Role of Women

Women were expected to marry and then devote themselves to making a happy home. In her book *Household Management*, Mrs Beeton informed young wives of their responsibilities.

A wife's duty is the promotion of happiness of others … to make sacrifices that his enjoying may be enhanced.

Mrs Beeton, 1861

In her book *Manners for Women*, aimed at middle-class women, 'Madge of Truth' (Mrs C E Humphry) said women should look 'shallow' and not be too clever.

A man likes his wife to be intelligent … but he is exasperated if she should be too intelligent. He does not like to be divined. His depths are to be inviolate; but he likes to sound her shallows; and so well does she know this that she often assumes a shallowness when she has it not.

Mrs C E Humphry, 1897

Here the woman's role in life is outlined by Alfred Tennyson, the Poet Laureate.

Man for the field and woman for the hearth;
Man for the sword and for the needle she;

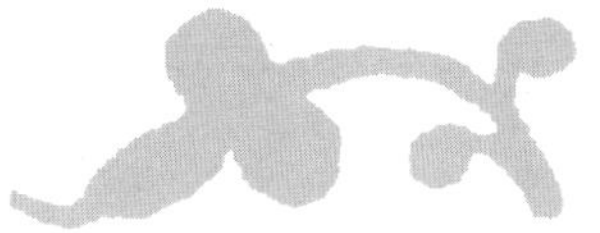

Man with the head and woman with the heart;
Man to command and woman to obey.

Alfred Tennyson, 1847

Most Victorians probably agreed with Tennyson, but many did not. Florence Nightingale, born into a wealthy family, rebelled against this idea. If women have a subordinate position in married life it stifles their freedom; it is not even truly loving.

And if a woman's music and drawing are only used by her as an amusement (a 'pass-time', as it is called), is it wonderful that she tires of them, that she becomes disgusted with them?... That man and woman have an equality of duties and rights is accepted by woman even less than by man. Behind his destiny woman must annihilate herself, must be only his complement. A woman dedicates herself to the vocation of her husband. She fills up and performs the subordinate parts of it. But if she has any destiny, any vocation of her own, she must renounce it, in nine cases out of ten.

Florence Nightingale, 1852

Mothering

It was very hard for poor people to bring up a family. Parents might give children up for adoption – sometimes to unsuitable people. This is an advertisement for children from a newspaper.

Adoption: A good home with a mother's love and care is offered to any respectable person wishing her child to be entirely adopted. Premuim £5[1] which includes everything. Apply by letter only.

Victorian advertisement, c. 1850

1. **£5**: about £275 in today's money. See page 13.

With little available birth control, Victorian mothers had many children. If they also had to work to feed the family, their own daughters often had to be, not just play, mother. George Sims, in *How the Poor Live,* described one 'little mother' in the London East End.

At the open door sits a girl of eight ... a typical 'little mother' of the London doorstep... She is nursing a heavy baby who is perhaps a year old. She talks to it, soothes it, hushes it to sleep, rocks it, dandles it when it wakes up, and kisses its poor little face again and again. But every other minute her attention is distracted by the conduct of her sister, aged four, and a brother, aged five, who are also under her guardianship.

George Sims, 1883

In many middle- and upper-class homes, women did not bring up their children in person, but organized others to do so. They started with the 'wet-nurse', a woman to feed the baby breast milk, and moved on to the nanny and the governess. Here the ideal wet-nurse is described.

Her breath should be sweet, and perspiration free from smell ... her teeth, white and perfect... Her milk should be white, inodorous, inclining to a sweet taste, neither watery nor thick, of moderate consistency, separating into curd over a slow fire.

The Mother's Medical Adviser, 1843

While the middle-class mother concerned herself with running her household, the working-class mother had a non-stop job to keep her family together. Joseph Corbett, a button burnisher, gave this description of his family life to a Parliamentary Select Committee in 1840.

My mother ... was married early. She became the mother of eleven children. I am the eldest. To the best of her ability she performed the important duties of a wife and mother.

She was lamentably deficient in domestic knowledge; in the most important of all human instruction, how to make the home and the fire-side to possess a charm for her husband and children, she had never received one single lesson.

Poor thing, the power to make the home cheerful and comfortable was never given to her. She knew not the value of cherishing in my father's mind a love of domestic objects. My heart aches when I reflect upon her anxious and labourious situation.

Forced to work in a shop in order to feed the family, Joseph's mother often stayed up all night to keep up with washing and mending clothes at home. His father became annoyed by this and spent time in the public house.

My mother's ignorance of household duties; my father's consequent irritability and intemperance; the frightful poverty; the constant quarrelling; the pernicious example to my brothers and sisters; the bad effect upon the future conduct of my brothers; one and all of us forced out to work, so young, that our feeble earnings would produce only 1 shilling[1] a week; cold and hunger, and the innumerable sufferings of my childhood, crowd upon my mind and overpower me.

Joseph Corbett, 1840

1. **shilling:** see page 13.
2. **knickers**: short trousers or shorts.

Children

George Noakes, in his autobiography, *To Be a Farmer's Boy,* remembered the clothes of a late-Victorian childhood.

We were all in skirts in those days. We only started to wear knickers[2] when we started school, so we all looked very much alike.

George Noakes, 1977

Dr Samuel Barker, in *The Domestic Management of Infants and Children in Health and Sickness,* advising parents on toys, recommended dolls for girls but not guns for boys.

It may be proper to caution parents against giving their children toys of a kind likely to encourage war-like or savage propensities: such as mimic guns, swords or other military accoutrements. We have remarked that toys of this kind are normally given to children in France, a practice which perhaps tends to nourish a love of war in our neighbours. We hope English parents will avoid this folly, and impart toys only of a simply amusing or improving tendency.

Dr Samuel Barker, 1875

Working-class children would be expected to help their parents a great deal around the house, with the shopping and looking after younger brothers and sisters. When they were free to play, many urban children played on the streets, as this woman from Bolton described in the 1880s.

The boys congregated in groups, particularly playing football and we – the younger element – had to be on guard for the bobby coming, because, you see, you were liable to be fined for playing football in the street in those days, you know.

Bolton resident, 1880s

Many working-class children had little time for play, as shown by this survey of London schools in 1897. On average these 8-9-year-old boys did 20 hours work a week - and many did over 40.

Little match-box makers work habitually from the time that school closes until eleven or even midnight.

London school survey, 1897

In Flora Thompson's family biography, *Lark Rise to Candleford,* she described the different prospects for boys and girls in a better off working-class home.

A soon as the little girl approached school leaving age, her mother would say, "About time you was earnin' your livin' me gal."... From that time onward the child was made to

feel herself one too many in the overcrowded home; while her brothers, when they left school and began to bring home a few shillings[1] weekly, were treated with a new consideration and made much of. The parents did not want the boys to leave home.

Flora Thompson, 1945

1. **shilling:** see page 13.

Home Comforts

A family's way of life varied greatly between regions and even within classes. Skilled workers, unlike the unskilled, might have parlours, or 'front rooms', housing all their best furniture. It was a crowded home life for Flora Thompson's family.

Often the big boys of a family slept downstairs, or were sent to sleep in the second bedroom of an elderly couple whose own children were out in the world. Except at holiday times, there were no big girls to provide for, as they were all out in service[2]. Still it was often a tight fit, for children swarmed, eight, ten or even more in some families, and although they were seldom all at home together, the eldest often being married before the youngest was born, beds and shakedowns were often so closely packed that the inmates had to climb over one bed to get into another.

Flora Thompson, 1945

2. **in service:** working as a household servant.

Many urban families lived in shocking conditions. The Town Clerk of Macclesfield described part of his town.

In four small cottages, with two bedrooms each and with two rooms on the ground floor, there was an average of 188 persons lodged. They had a small yard, and the remains only of what had been two privies[3], all the ordure being in the open yard.

In another lodging house near, there were three small rooms upstairs: in the first were 16 men, women and children, lying together on the floor; in the second there were twelve, also on the floor; and the third room upstairs was used as a

3. **privy:** an outside lavatory.

privy, the boarded floor being literally covered with human ordure.

Clerk's Report, 1850s

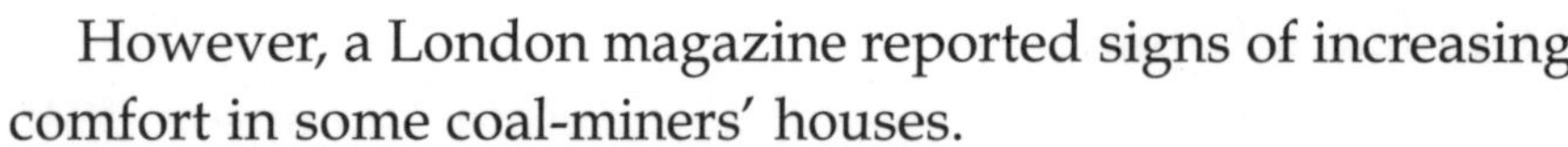

However, a London magazine reported signs of increasing comfort in some coal-miners' houses.

In the best ordered pit dwellings I have often seen also good chairs, china, bright brass candlesticks, and chimney ornaments; every one of these items being kept scrupulously clean, for cleanliness is the pride of the pitman's wife.

The Illustrated London News, 1860s

The social reformer B Seebohm Rowntree, studying poverty and town life in York at the end of the Victorian period, described the living room of 'well-to-do artisans', who made up 12 per cent of the working class of the city.

The real living-room is the kitchen, rendered cheerful and homely by the large open grate and the good oven, unknown in the south, but familiar in the north of England where coal is cheap. The floor of this room is commonly covered with linoleum, although a large home-made hearth-rug may lend an air of solid comfort. A sofa, albeit of horsehair or American cloth, and china ornaments on the high mantelpiece, add the subtle touch of homeliness.

B Seebohm Rowntree, 1901

Servants

Middle-class and upper-class homes were run by an army of household servants who made up a large proportion of the working population – 13 per cent in 1851 and 16 per cent in 1891. Many young women in service[1] worked non-stop. How did Hannah Cullick have time to write a diary?

1st Jan. 1871 – This is the beginning of another year, and I am still general servant like, to Mrs Henderson at 20 Gloucester Crescent. This month... if I live till the

1. **in service**: see page 41.

26 o' May when I shall be 38-year-old, I shall o' bin in service 30 years... Anything as wants strength or height I am sent for or called up to do it. All the cabs that's wanted I get, and if the young ladies want fetching or taking anywhere, I've to walk with them and carry their cloaks or parcels. I clean all the copper scuttles and dig the coals, clean the tins and help to clean the silver and do the washing up if I'm wanted, and carry things up as far as the door for dinner. I clean four grates and do the fires and the flags and area railings and all that in the street. I clean the water-closet and privy[2] out and the backyard and the area, the back stairs and the passage, the larder, pantry and boy's room and the kitchen and scullery, all the cupboards downstairs and them in the storeroom. And after the house-cleaning I do the walls down from the top to the bottom of the house and clean all the high paint, and dust the pictures. I get all the meals down stairs and lay the cloth and wait on the boy and the housemaid as much as they want and if it's my work, like changing their plates and washing their knives and forks and that.

Hannah Cullick, 1871

2. **privy**: see page 41.

Servants needed to know their place in society, and their manners. This *Servants' Behaviour Book* gave some basic rules.

Never begin to talk to your mistress, unless it be to deliver a message, or ask a necessary question.

Nuresmaids are often encouraged to sing in the nursery; but they should leave off immediately on the entrance of a lady or gentleman.

I have seen servants make the mistake of going to walk or sit in the garden, as if it were a part of the house belonging to them.

Never take a small thing into a room in your hand. Any small thing should be handed on a little tray, silver or not, kept for the purpose.

Servants' Behaviour Book, 1850s

Education

There was no free state education at the start of Victoria's reign, but there were schools for those who could afford to pay for them. There were 'dame' schools where very small children were looked after and perhaps taught. There were private day schools, factory schools and Sunday schools.

Wealthy families could afford to educate their children at home, generally with a governess. Many boys were sent to public schools when they were 13, to pursue their education further. Poorer children often received no education at all because their parents couldn't afford to pay for it, and they needed the children to work for money from a young age.

The quality of education was generally poor as teachers did not need qualifications, and books and equipment were often scarce. Gradually laws changed so that by 1880 it was compulsory for all children to attend school between the ages of 5 and 10. Many MPs and other social leaders continued to campaign for better education for all.

Schools and Teachers

From 1839, inspectors were appointed to report about standards in schools, with a bid to improve them. This report was made by an inspector who visited a 'private' school at the back of a shop. These private schools often charged low fees and were attended by the children of the poor.

I was directed to a room in the rear of a shop, about ten feet by twelve, in which, with my hat on, I could barely stand upright. The floor was crowded with benches, on which some dozen children were sitting in ranks closely packed, many without any means of employing their time. The mistress was in the shop, having left the children in the care of a girl who was standing amidst the crowd with an infant in her arms.

School Report, 1843

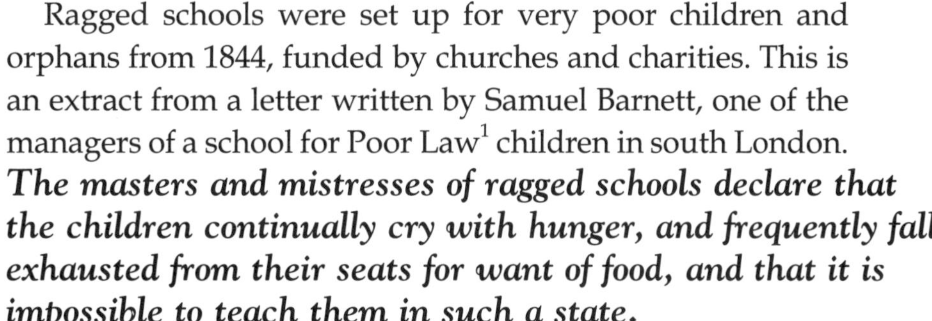

1. **Poor Law**: the body of laws in Britain developed to provide relief for the poor.
2. **apprentice system**: when a person learns their trade or skill while working for the person training them.

Ragged schools were set up for very poor children and orphans from 1844, funded by churches and charities. This is an extract from a letter written by Samuel Barnett, one of the managers of a school for Poor Law[1] children in south London.

The masters and mistresses of ragged schools declare that the children continually cry with hunger, and frequently fall exhausted from their seats for want of food, and that it is impossible to teach them in such a state.

Samuel Barnett, 1868

Victorian governments became concerned about poor schooling. In 1842, a Council on Education met to discuss it. A serious problem was teachers' pay, said one speaker.

If the village schoolmaster be worse paid than the village carpenter or blacksmith, what hope is there of finding any but the most incompetent person in the former situation?

Council of Education, 1842

Reverand Bellairs, a contributor to a Council on Education in 1847-8, believed that the apprentice system[2] could be used to train teachers.

Benefits would arise if such scholars as might be distinguished by proficiency and good conduct were apprenticed to skilful masters, to be instructed and trained, so as to be prepared to complete their education as schoolmasters in a Normal School.

Minutes, Committee of the Council on Education, 1847-8

Victorian teachers were paid by 'results' – which meant according to how well children answered inspectors' questions. An ex-pupil remembered this 1860s visit.

Two inspectors came once a year and carried out a dramatic examination. The schoolmaster came into school in his best suit; all the pupils and teachers would be listening, till at ten o'clock a dog-cart would be heard on the road, even

though it was 80 yards [73 metres] away. In would come two gentlemen with a deportment of high authority, with rich voices. Each would sit at a desk and children would be called in turn to one or the other. The master hovered round, calling children out as they were needed. The children could see him start with vexation as a good pupil stuck at a word in the reading book he had been using all the year, or sat motionless with his sum in front of him. The master's anxiety was deep, for his earnings depended on the children's work. One year the atmosphere so affected the lower standards that, one after another as they were brought to the Inspector, the boys howled and the girls whimpered. It took hours to get through them.

Recollection of an 1860s school child, c. 1900

Samuel Barnett described the improvements that took place in the school he managed between 1875 and 1885.

The children were not called by their names. Each was commonly addressed as 'child'. They had no toys, no library, no Sunday School, no places in which to keep personal possessions, no playing-fields, no night garments, no prizes, no flowers, no pots, no pictures on the walls, no pleasures in music, no opportunities for seeing the world outside the school walls...

Ten years later...

... the children romped in playing-fields, dug and delved in little gardens, talked busily at meals, wore night garments, owned three sets of apparel; possessed toys, large ones, in common; small treasures, such as dolls, puzzle books and boxes, which now live in personally owned lockers... Bare rooms had been decorated with pictures... Flowers grew in the windows, cats kittened in the laundry, canaries sang... Each girl was called by her Christian prefix[1]. Each boy by his sire's name[2].

Samuel Barnett, 1875-1885

1. **Christian prefix:** first name.
2. **sire's name:** surname.

Support for Schooling

Some employers and property owners resisted education for the poor, believing that it would encourage workers to 'get above themselves' and demand higher wages and more political rights. Many working-class parents could not afford for their children to be at school, rather than earning money at work. When the 20 Hours Bill was presented in Parliament, there were objections from employers of children.

There was a bill for making it compulsory on the employers of the labour of children under 12 years old, to have a certificate that the child was learning to read and write, and had twenty hours of teaching a month – nothing like an hour a day. But so monstrous an innovation frightened the House. Mr Henley ... said that people were not to eat unless they worked, but were not commanded to read and write. Mr Buxton ... said there were thousands of children too idle, wicked or stupid to learn... Mr Hardy said that the children of the poor were taught quite enough to enable them to do the duties they were intended for.

Punch, 1860

In the countryside, there was often not much support for the idea, as a Commission on Popular Education discovered.

Farmers seldom feel any interest in the school, and seldom therefore subscribe to it. As a class the landowners, especially those who are non-resident [though there are many honourable exceptions] do not do their duty in the support of popular education.

Commission on Popular Education, 1861

Some reformers wanted good schools for everyone. The National Education League demanded free, compulsory, non-church schools. Its leader, Joseph Chamberlain, wrote this.

More schools are required, and the regular attendance of children must be secured. Neither of these ... is attainable

without compulsion. In the present state of religious parties, no agreement as to a common theological[1] instruction can be arrived at, therefore the schools must be thoroughly unsectarian[2]. Lastly they must be free.

Joseph Chamberlain, 1870

1. **theological**: religious.
2. **unsectarian**: not linked with a particular branch of Christianity.

By late Victorian times, new girls-only schools had begun to open, in response to a middle-class demand for good education for girls. However, many people, including women like this one, continued to think that education at home was best for girls.

I am obliged to you for your letter respecting the proposed college for Ladies, but as I have decided objections to bringing large masses of girls together and think that home education under the inspection and encouragement of sensible fathers, or voluntarily continued by the girls themselves, is far more valuable than any external education. I am afraid I cannot help you... All the most superior women I have known have thus been formed by home influence.

Charlotte Yonge, 1870

What Children Learnt

There was a strong prejudice against girls doing much academic work. This late Victorian Board School Report said that girls are better off learning domestic skills.

A girl is not necessarily a better woman because she knows the height of all the mountains in Europe, and can work a fraction in her head; but she is decidedly better fitted for the duties she will be called upon to perform in life if she knows how to wash and tend a child, cook simple food well, and thoroughly clean a house.

School Report, 1874

A Noun is the name of a

-HAD-A-LITTLE-
NVT-TREE

In the 1890s, Gwen Raverat's brothers were at 'public' schools, schools for wealthy middle- and upper-class boys, where the curriculum was mainly Classics.

What Tom learned at Shrewsbury was clear enough – Latin and Greek, with the ancient history and geography pertaining to them. The only English literature that reached him were lines to be put into Latin verse, while Milton was used for punishment. There is a pencil note in his copy of **Paradise Lost**[3]***: "Had to write 500 lines of this for being caught reading*** **King Lear**[4] ***in class." The only modern geography he knew was a map of Scotland, because this too was chosen as a punishment.***

Gwen Raverat, c. 1910-1920

3. ***Paradise Lost***: an epic poem by John Milton.
4. ***King Lear***: a play by William Shakespeare.

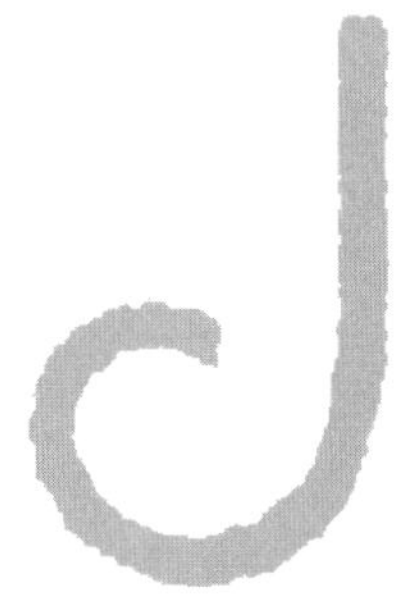

Mary Hughes described some 1880s rules at the North London Collegiate in her book *A London Girl of the Eighties.*

No girl might bring a pen to school. We were forbidden to get wet on the way to school, to walk more than three in a row, to drop a pencil box, leave a book at home, run down the stairs, speak in class.

Mary Hughes, 1936

Some of the school rules at Cheltenham Ladies College, a fee-paying school for girls, were stern.

Leave must be asked from the class teacher before speaking to another pupil.

Leave must be obtained from both class teachers before speaking to a pupil in another class.

Conversations must be finished in the place where permission is given and may not be carried on in dressing rooms, corridors or staircases.

Cheltenham Ladies College, 1880s

thing

Religion and the Church

For many wealthy and middle-class Victorians, religion formed a central part of their lives. They regularly attended church and religion shaped the way they saw their own society.

Poorer people had begun to drift away from the Anglican Church, the established Church of England, in favour of the non-conformist[1] Methodist and Baptist churches founded in the 18th century. Even still, middle-class Victorians were shocked by the results of a census of church-attendance that was carried out in 1851. It recorded the fact that only 7 million out of a total population of 18 million went to church or chapel at all, and of them, 2 million were attending services away from the Anglican Church.

1. **non-conformist**: branches of Christianity which are Protestant but have broken away from the established Church of England.

Attending Church and Chapel

For many Victorian families, particularly the wealthier ones, Sunday was a sacred day of prayer and rest. Some families went to church twice in one day. Mary Hughes remembered services at St Paul's Cathedral in the 1880s. Listening to sermons and readings from the Bible was part of the family's way of life; she and her brother did not ask questions when they were puzzled.

How cool and vast the cathedral seemed after the dusty streets! We walked with precision to our special seats, for the vergers knew us well. My father had a stall, my brothers sat in a pew beyond the choir, my mother and I sat in the reserved front row under the dome.

Later...

Like all children I put some kind of meaning into the strange Prayer Book phrases. "The Scripture moveth us in sundry places" must mean that it pokes us in various parts of our body – a spiritual dig in the ribs: "Come on now, own up."... Walking home with Barnholt, I asked him what "begotten[2]" meant. He wasn't quite sure, but thought it was pretty much the same as "forgotten". I was satisfied, and never

2. **begotten**: generated or created.

pushed any farther, concluding that to be the only one "forgotten" was just one of those odd things that happened to Jesus... After a sermon on Solomon's vision I asked Barnholt whether he would have chosen wisdom if he had been Solomon. "Oh no," he said, "I've got enough of that. I should have asked for a new cricket-bat."

Mary Hughes, 1936

Yet Andrew Mearns, in his pamphlet called *The Bitter Cry of Outcast London - An Enquiry into Condition of Abject Poor,* found that very few poor people went to any church or chapel. Sunday was the only day off for many working-class families.

One street off Leicester Square contains 246 families, and only 12 of these are ever represented at the house of God. In another street in Pentonville, out of 100 families only 12 persons attend any sanctuary[3], whilst the number of attendants [church-goers] in one district of St George's-in-the-East is 39 persons out of 4235... Constantly we come across persons who have never been to a church or chapel for 20 years ... and some persons as old as 64 have never been in a place of worship at all.

3. **sanctuary**: place of worship.

Andrew Mearns, 1883

The religious census of 1851 suggested why so many millions were 'missing' from church.

One chief cause of the dislike which the labouring population entertains for religious services is thought to be the maintenance of those distinctions by which they are separated as a class from the class above them. Working men, it is contended, cannot enter our religious structures without having pressed on their notice some memento of inferiority. The existence of pews and the position of the free seats are, it is said, alone sufficient to deter them from our churches, and religion has thus come to be regarded as a purely middle-class property or luxury.

Religious census, 1851

came to vi - sit me, And all for the sake of my lit -tle r

Religious Feeling

In towns, the middle classes especially were regular church-goers and believers. They observed Sunday as a day of rest and quiet. Daily family prayers were a common custom, whether taken casually or seriously. This passage relates to the 1880s.

Family prayers, which my dear old grandfather had treated sketchily, were carried out by Uncle Bill with relentless thoroughness. Instead of mumbling a few requests to the Almighty, as grandpapa did, he acquired a book which covered the whole nation in its petitions, and even, on Fridays, went the length of praying for foreigners. All the servants were assembled, and it was morning and evening.

Mary Hughes, 1936

The writer Somerset Maugham was born in 1874. One of his stories has this 'man's' view of the value of church-going.

A man wants a wife who can cook his dinner and look after his children. I've tried both and I know. I make a point of the children going to Sunday school and I like Betty to go to church. I think women ought to be religious. I don't believe myself, but I like a woman and children to.

Somerset Maugham, c. 1920

But for many religion was a matter of faith and genuine belief. Methodist minister William Booth felt so strongly that the established religion was neglecting the poor and working class that he began his own Christian Mission in 1865, renaming it the Salvation Army in 1878. He believed in using popular music to spread the Christian message:

Secular music, do you say, belongs to the devil? Does it? Well, if it did I would plunder him for it, for he has no right to a single note of the whole seven... Every note, and every strain, and every harmony is divine, and belongs to us... So consectrate your voice and your instruments. Bring out your

cornets and harps and organs and flutes and violins and pianos and drums, and everything else that can make melody. Offer them to God, and use them to make all the hearts about you merry before the Lord.

William Booth, 1880

Singing Hymns

The Salvation Army was not the only Christian group to use music to inspire its followers. The Victorian period was a great time for hymns - composing them and singing them. Some of these appealed to the faithful to fight for their beliefs:

Onward, Christian soldiers,
Marching as to war,
With the Cross of Jesus
Going on before!

Sabine Baring-Gould, 1864

Others were more reflective, such as this verse from the beautiful carol by the poet Christina Rossetti.

In the bleak mid-winter
Frosty wind made moan,
Earth stood hard as iron,
Water like a stone;
Snow had fallen, snow on snow
Snow on snow,
In the bleak mid-winter
Long ago.

Christina Rossetti, 1862

Health and Medicine

In health and medicine, the Victorian era had two faces. It was a time of great advances, but also a time of great misery and ill-health.

One kind of advance was in insights and inventions. The discovery that chloroform could be used as an anaesthetic in 1847 and the invention of a carbolic acid germicide in 1865 meant that there were many fewer deaths from surgery. Innoculations against smallpox and diptheria were developed, saving thousands of lives.

The second kind of advance was to realise that public health needed tackling head on. Edwin Chadwick's report into the *Sanitary Condition of the Labouring Population* in 1842 was funded by the government. With the establishment of the civil service, large-scale investigations could be made into the causes of ill-health, and reforms followed. The Public Health Act of 1848 dealt with sewers and drains and, from then on, steady attempts were made to make life less unhealthy and unsafe.

Overcrowding and Urban Living

Poor people in industrial towns lived, on average, much shorter lives than any other group of people. In a Poor Law[1] Commission Report, Edwin Chadwick provided these figures for 1842.

Average age of Death	*Manchester*	*Rutland*
Professional Persons and gentry and families	38	52
Tradesmen and families [inc. farmers in Rutland]	20	41
Mechanics, labourers and their families	17	38

Poor Law Commission Report, 1842

1. **Poor Law**: see page 45.

For great numbers of people, ill-health, overcrowding and bad living conditions went together. Edwin Chadwick's report into living conditions shocked many people and reforms followed. This section of the report described poor houses in Leeds.

... broken panes in every window-frame, and filth and vermin in every nook. With the walls unwhitewashed for years, black with the smoke of foul chimneys, without water ... with sacking for bedding, with floors unwashed from year to year ... can we wonder that such places are the hot-beds of disease?... The annual loss from filth and bad ventilation is greater than the loss from death and wounds in any wars in which the country has been engaged in modern times.

After listing changes he wished to see made (by Parliament), he made this claim:

By combinations of all these arrangements, it is probable that ... an increase of 13 years [of life] at least may be extended to the whole of the working classes.

Edwin Chadwick, 1842

2. **cholera**: see page 4.

Between 1846-49, 50,000 people in England and Wales died of cholera[2], a water-borne disease. In 1848, the link between filthy water and poor health was officially admitted by the Public Health Act that set about improving sewers and drains over the whole land. How bad the state of non-sanitation was in early Victorian times can be seen from this description in *The Leeds Intelligence* of the River Aire – which supplied the city's drinking-water.

S

It is charged with the contents of about 200 water-closets and similar places, a great number of common drains, the drainings from dunghills, the Infirmary [dead leeches, poultices for patients, etc.], slaughter houses, chemical soap, gas, dung, dyehouses and manufactories, spent black and blue dye, pig manure, old urine wash, with all sorts of decomposed animal and vegetable substances from an extent

of drainage, amounting to about 30,000,000 gallons per annum of the mass of filth with which the river is loaded.

The Leeds Intelligence, 1841

Work and Health

There was plenty of evidence linking factory work with deformity and ill-health but doctors often did not want to see it. The Inspecting Surgeon for Preston is being quoted here in a speech in Parliament in 1844; the speaker did not want working hours for children reduced.

I have not met with a single instance, out of 1,656 children whom I examined, of deformity that is referable to factory labour. It must be admitted that factory children do not present the same blooming, robust appearance as is witnessed among children who labour in the open air; but I question if they are not more exempt from acute disease, and do not, on the whole, suffer less sickness than those who are regarded as having more healthy employment.

Mr Harrison, 1844

But others had seen a 'deterioration in personal form' – like bowing of the legs – amongst factory workers. Peter Gaskell, an apothecary and a member of the Royal College of Surgeons, wrote this in his book *The Manufacturing Population of England*.

Their stature, low – the average height of 400 men, measured at different places ... being 5 feet 6 inches [165 cm]. Their limbs slender, and playing out badly and ungracefully. A very general bowing of the legs. Great numbers of girls and women walking lamely or awkwardly, with raised chests and spinal flexures. Nearly all have flat feet...

Peter Gaskell, 1833

Safer Operations

Scientists made important discoveries during this time. Anaesthetics, using chloroform, were used for the first time. Joseph Lister, a surgeon working in the Glasgow Infirmary, discovered that the germs that he believed caused gangrene could be killed by carbolic acid so surgical operation became safer. Carbolic acid became known as antiseptic. He refers to a boy who 'got entangled with a machine'.

Without the assistance of the antiseptic treatment, I should certainly have thought of nothing else but amputation at the shoulder joint; but ... as the fingers had sensation, I did not hesitate to try to save the limb, and adopted the treatment described. The boy continued free from unfavourable symptoms, while the limb remained free from swelling, redness or pain... The severest forms of wounds heal thus kindly under the antiseptic treatment.

Joseph Lister, 1865

Disease and illness were everywhere. If you did fall ill, going to hospital could actually kill you, as Florence Nightingale writes in *Notes on Nursing*. A year later the Nightingale Training School for Nurses was opened at St Thomas' Hospital, London, as a result of Florence's campaign to have nursing taken seriously as a profession.

If a patient is cold, if a patient is feverish, if a patient is faint, if he is sick after taking food, if he has a bed-sore, it is generally the fault not of the disease, but of the nursing... By this I do not mean that the nurse is always to blame. Bad sanitary, bad architectural, and bad administrative arrangements often make it impossible to nurse.

Florence Nightingale, 1859

Sports and Pastimes

Many wealthy Victorians lived off income from land or inherited wealth so they had much leisure time, for social visiting, weekend house-parties, hunting and cultural visits. The middle classes copied their 'betters', if they could afford it, or were accepted socially. They held musical evenings where the talented guests were called upon to entertain everyone with poetry readings and musical performances. They also played croquet, golf, cricket, and the newer games of rugby and lawn tennis.

Many working people had no time for leisure at all but the prosperity of the age did filter down and many families were better off at the end of the era than at the beginning. Working men took part in some sporting activities, especially boxing, cricket and football. But they had their own pastimes, too, like pigeon-fancying. Horse-racing became more popular.

Upper-class Pastimes

Anna Fray, a young American visiting her English uncle in Shropshire, reported the conversation at an upper-class dinner table. The conversation included the previous day's hunting and shooting.

Naturally the conversation turns upon the day's sport, and you hear how that bird was wing'd: how another was tailered; how many cock pheasants were shot; how many hen pheasants were deprived of life; how many woodcock were put up; how many partridges flew out of one cover; how many rabbits were killed; who shot well; who shot badly; who missed fire; whose cock pheasant fell with his tail up, whose hen pheasant with her tail down, who shot on this side the dingle, who the other, and so forth, and so forth, and so on.

Anna Fray, 1851

Motoring became an upper-class pastime in late Victorian times. Cars were very expensive. A woman's diary of the time

reveals the adventure of motoring.

Dec 9 Drove to Lee at ten. Motor sparked at once and went well. After lunch started for home in motor car; came round by Fareham; had lovely drive; police spotted us; awful crowd followed us at Cosham; had to beat them off with umbrella.
Dec 10 Policeman called at 10.30, took our names re driving through Fareham without red flag[1] ahead.
Dec 27 Frightened an unattended horse attached to a milkcart, which bolted and sent the milk cans flying in all directions.
Jan 4 Lost nut off air valve; pushed home.

Diary, 1893

1. **red flag**: by law, car drivers were required to drive no faster than four miles an hour in built-up areas and a man had to walk in front waving a red flag.

Leisure for All

Henry Mayhew spent many years talking to and observing the poor, at work and in their leisure hours. His work revealed to many Victorians unpleasant hidden parts of their world. This extract is from a long account of an evening's 'ratting'.

Preparation now began for the grand match of the evening, in which fifty rats were to be killed... This match seemed to be between the proprietor and his son, and the stake to be gained was only a bottle of lemonade. It was strange to see the daring manner in which the lad introduced his hand into the rat cage as he fumbled about and stirred up with his fingers the living mass, picking up, as he had been requested, 'only the big uns'.

Henry Mayhew, c. 1851

Many of the parks we enjoy today were laid out in the Victorian era. In 1889, Sydney H Waterlow donated his entire estate of 29 acres in Highgate to the London County Council to establish a public park for the benefit of labourers in North London, as related in a letter to the chairman of the London County Council.

This latter object [the creation of public parks] can, I think, be best accomplished by the kindness of individuals acting through the agency of the London County Council, and with as little burden as possible on the public rates. Therefore, to assist in providing large 'gardens for the gardenless,' and as an expression of attachment to the great city in which I have worked for fifty-three years, I desire to present to the Council, as a free gift, my entire interest in the estate at Highgate... I will, in addition, pay over to the Council the sum of £6,000 in cash ... this sum of money to be used in ... defraying the cost of laying out the estate as a public park in perpetuity as the Council may deem most desirable.

Sydney H Waterlow, 1889

In late Victorian times, respectable middle-class people sometimes disapproved of country pleasures, believing they were a waste of time and money. Alfred Williams, who lived in the upper Thames area, saw these pleasures threatened.

The village fair and club festival were condemned because simple folk people assembled together to indulge in simple amusements. The sight of so many 'poor foolish' peasant folk thronging the streets ... laughing immoderately at the antics of a fifth-rate clown, or gaping at the Punch and Judy show, or dancing together at the old fiddler sitting on the ground, or throwing at the 'knock 'em downs', or bowling at the 'milky cocoa-nuts', was an offence to those who affected a superiority of taste.

Alfred Williams, 1910

Though many Victorians came to disapprove of drink, the public house was an important part of village life. In *Lark Rise to Candleford,* Flora Thompson described the taproom of 'The Wagon and Horses' pub – in late Victorian Oxfordshire.

There the adult male population gathered every evening, to sip its half-pints, drop by drop, to make them last, and to

discuss local events, wrangle over politics or farming methods, or to sing a few songs 'to oblige'... It was exclusively a men's gathering.

Flora Thompson, 1945

Cycling became an extraordinarily popular weekend pastime. Gwen Raverat, a grand-daughter of Charles Darwin, described Darwin's reaction to women on bicycles.

Two ladies – or as grandpa says, two shameless females – in bloomers[1] bicycled through the village yesterday, and some of the women were so scandalized that they threw stones at them. I didn't dare to say so but I thought they looked very neat, though I don't think I should like to show my own legs to the world like that.

Gwen Raverat, c. 1910-1920

1. **bloomers**: wide trousers designed by a Mrs Bloomer.

Going to the theatre and music-hall was a popular Victorian pastime. Charles Dickens loved the theatre. This is from *The Old Curiosity Shop*.

The lady ... the tyrant ... the man who sung the song with the lady's maid and danced the chorus ... the pony who reared up on his hind legs when he saw the murderer ... the clown who ventured on such familiarities with the military man in boots ... the lady who jumped over the nine and twenty ribbons and came down safe on the horse's back.

Charles Dickens, 1840

Another increasingly popular pastime, made possible by easy rail-travel, was sea-bathing. Poorer people went for the day, the wealthy for long holidays.

The beach where the machines are placed from ten till one or two o'clock is so crowded with ladies and gentlemen that it is difficult to walk through the throng, especially if it be nearly high water. The visitors are close to the machines. The water is black with bathers.

The Observer, 1856

Timeline

1837-1901 Reign of Queen Victoria.
1837 London Men's Working Association demands reforms including the vote for all. Euston railway station opens. Charles Dickens' *Oliver Twist* begins as a serial in *Bentley's Miscellany*.
1838-48 Chartist Movement active.
1838 First steamboat crossing of the Atlantic.
1839 Opium War with China. First railway timetables. Charles Darwin publishes research based on his voyage on *HMS Beagle*.
1840 Penny Post introduced by Rowland Hill. Maori chiefs surrender 'New Zealand'. Chimney Sweeps Act.
1841 Thomas Cook's first railway excursions.
1842 Edwin Chadwick's *Report on Sanitary Condition of the Labouring Population* is published. Ashley's Mines Act.
1844 Factory Act – 12-hour day for women; 6-hour day for children between the ages of 8 and 13.
1845-50 Famine in Ireland.
1846 Edward Lear writes his *Book of Nonsense*. The first public parks outside London open in Manchester
1847 Charlotte Bronte's *Jane Eyre*, Anne Bronte's *Agnes Grey* and Emily Bronte's *Wuthering Heights* are all published.
1849 Cholera epidemic in London. 14,000 die. Robert Stephenson's cast-iron bridge over the River Tyne at Newçastle was completed. His tubular bridge over the Menai Straits opened for rail traffic.
1850 Alfred Tennyson was made Poet Laureate.
1851 Australian Gold Rush. Great Exhibition in London.
1853-56 Crimean War.
1855 Bessemer invents process for turning iron into steel.
1857 Divorce courts set up in England and Wales.
1858 Irish Republican Brotherhood is founded. London's 'Great Stink'.
1859 First overseas cricket tour – to Canada.
1860 First Food and Drugs Act – to punish adulteration of foods.
1861 Death of Albert, Prince Consort. Thomas Cook's first continental holiday tour – to Paris.
1864 Gladstone supports parliamentary reform – with votes for all men.
1865 Road Locomotion Act. Top speed, 4 mph.

Road locomotives (cars) require three attendants, one with red flag walking in front.
1867 Rebellion in Ireland.
Second Parliamentary Reform Act – now nearly all men in towns could vote.
Dr Barnardo opened children's shelter in Stepney.
1868 First Trades Union Congress meets.
1869 John Stewart Mill publishes *Subjection of Women*.
1870 Married Women's Property Act – wives can now own their own property.
Education Act – accepts that basic schooling for all is a government responsibility.
1871 Lewis Carroll publishes *Through the Looking Glass*.
Rugby Football Union founded.
First Bank Holiday.
First hall of residence for women established at Girton College, Cambridge.
1872 Ballot Act – voting becomes secret. First international football match.
Thomas Hardy publishes *Under the Greenwood Tree*.
1877 Proclamation of Empire of India, Victoria Empress.
First tennis championship at All England Club, Wimbledon.
1879 Tay Bridge Disaster.
Electric lighting on Waterloo bridge.
Joseph Lister describes his antiseptic treatment to fellow doctors.
1880 Parnell urges Irish peasants to shun cleared land.
1882 Electric trams in London area.
1884 Royal Commission on Housing of Working Classes is set up.
Third Parliamentary Reform Act – same rights are given to male voters in towns and countryside.
1886 First Irish Home Rule Bill is defeated.
1888 Football League met.
Lawn Tennis Association is formed.
1890 First underground electric railway in world opened – in London.
1891 Telephone linked London and Paris.
Education Act – fees for elementary schooling are abolished.
1892 Second Irish Home Rule Bill.
1894 Women get the vote in council elections.
1896 Queen filmed in first royal movie.
1900 Mines Act – no children under 13 to work in the pits.
1901 Death of Queen Victoria – accession of King Edward VII.

Index